The Senior Patrol Leader Handbook

BOY SCOUTS OF AMERICA®

32501A
ISBN 0-8395-2501-X
©2007 Boy Scouts of America

Contents

Welcome!

With three green bars behind the Scout

emblem, the senior patrol leader's shoulder patch is one of the oldest symbols in Scouting. The Boy Scouts of America has long recognized the senior patrol leader as the highest youth leadership position in a troop. He is the primary link between a troop's Scouts and its adult leaders. He shoulders the responsibility for leading meetings of the troop and the patrol leaders' council. He provides valuable leadership in planning and carrying out the troop's program of outdoor activities, service projects, and events.

Now you have agreed to wear the senior patrol leader patch on the sleeve of your uniform. You have been elected by your fellow Scouts to help them make the most of their Scouting experiences.

Have confidence that this is a responsibility you can handle, and that you will be able to do it well. The troop members who elected you to this position have seen much in you that has convinced them you will be a good leader. You were elected because your fellow Scouts trusted you and believe that you will help the troop be successful and help them have a better Scouting experience. Good leaders accept leadership roles because they want to make a difference. Good leaders are servant leaders. They focus on helping others succeed.

You probably have many leadership skills already, and quite a bit of experience

using them. Perhaps you have served as a patrol leader. You may have played key roles in the success of Scout hikes and campouts. No doubt your efforts were important to patrol and troop service projects. You certainly have done your part to help make patrol and troop meetings run smoothly and well.

As senior patrol leader, you can continue to develop leadership skills that you will use for the rest of your life. You will be challenged many times in the coming months, but you also will find much satisfaction in the successes of the troop. When you look back upon your tenure as senior patrol leader, you may well remember this as among the most exciting times in your Scouting career.

Begin by thinking about your vision for the troop. What does success look like? What goals do you need to set to get there? When will you begin to develop your plans with the patrol leaders' council to accomplish those goals?

You have what it takes to be a good senior patrol leader. Draw on your strengths, be open to new ideas, and put your heart into it with the goal of making the troop the best it can be. Most of all, enjoy the opportunity to put your own special mark on a successful troop program.

Senior Patrol Leader Qualifications

1

Senior Patrol Leader Qualifications

Each troop sets its own age, rank, and
other qualification standards for its senior patrol leader, though these
may be temporarily waived if a troop is newly organized. A senior
patrol leader serves from one troop election to the next, usually
for a period of six to 12 months. In most troops, voting is done by
secret ballot. All youth members of the troop are eligible to vote.

The senior patrol leader of an established troop is often
selected from among the most experienced Scouts of a certain age
and rank. In a new troop or a troop without older members, Scouts
are likely to choose as senior patrol leader someone they respect
and believe will provide effective leadership.

Scouts in the troop can hardly wait to go on hikes, sleep in
tents, and cook meals in the open. They are eager to master
the skills of Scouting and to put into practice what they are
learning. They want to share experiences with their friends.

Challenge, adventure, leadership, recognition, growth—the
expectations boys bring to Scouting can be fulfilled. You
can help the members of the troop pull together the pieces
and make the BSA program come to life. Along the way, you
will discover that your own Scouting experience is greatly
enriched by serving as the troop's senior patrol leader.

As senior patrol leader, you will not be a member of a patrol, but you may participate in high-adventure activities with the troop's Venture patrol.

The patrol leaders' council may offer candidates for senior patrol leader the opportunity to appear before the troop to discuss their qualifications and reasons for seeking the office. This provides good practice for the candidates and enables those who do not know them well, younger Scouts in particular, to gain a better sense of what they propose to do for the troop.

Duties of a Senior Patrol Leader

While you are senior patrol leader, the troop is going to count upon you to live up to some clear expectations:

- Run all troop meetings, events, activities, and the annual program planning conference.

- Chair meetings of the patrol leaders' council.

- Appoint troop members to serve in the troop's other youth leader positions (with the advice and counsel of the Scoutmaster).

- Delegate duties and responsibilities to other youth leaders.

- Assist the Scoutmaster with troop leadership training.

- Set a good example.

- Wear the Scout uniform correctly.

- Show Scout spirit.

Being a good senior patrol leader will require a significant commitment of time. Consider all of your obligations to family, school, and religion, and find an appropriate balance, even if that means temporarily putting aside some extracurricular activities.

Your Support Group

As senior patrol leader, you will want to do your best to help the troop succeed. You are the point man, up front at meetings, delegating responsibilities for troop activities, and encouraging the patrols to accomplish all they can.

You are not in this alone, though. Scouting provides you with a group of adults and other youth leaders eager to help you succeed.

Adults with whom you will be working include those holding the following positions:

- Scoutmaster
- Assistant Scoutmaster
- Troop committee member
- Chartered organization representative

As senior patrol leader, you can expect the following from the troop's adult leaders:

- They will provide direction, coaching, and support.
- They will be available to help answer your questions.
- They will listen to your ideas.
- They will be fair.
- They will serve as good examples.
- They will offer advice when appropriate.
- They will back you on reasonable leadership decisions.

Being senior patrol leader goes beyond troop meeting nights. As the troop's youth leader with the greatest responsibilities, you can represent Scouting's best during troop events and in your school and community.

The Scoutmaster

As you gain experience as a senior patrol leader, you will find tremendous assistance and support from the Scoutmaster. The Scoutmaster's responsibility is to ensure that the troop program delivers the promise of Scouting, that the values of the Scout Oath and Law come to life in the troop, that the troop's leaders are developed, and that the environment for character development and fun is offered for every Scout. Make no mistake, the troop's leadership starts with the Scoutmaster. His is not a passive role, even though most of his work is done behind the scenes in support of your role. Adults are responsible to provide leadership to a boy-run troop.

A Scoutmaster trains boys to be leaders, makes available to them the resources and guidance they need to lead well, and then steps into the background and lets them do their jobs.

Rely on the Scoutmaster to coach you from the sidelines and to give you plenty of space to step before the troop and provide the active leadership Scouts expect from you. Do not hesitate to ask questions when you are unsure of what to do next. Share your concerns and successes with the Scoutmaster, and expect guidance in learning more effective ways to conduct troop activities and meetings. The Scoutmaster will always be there to give you the help you need.

The Assistant Scoutmasters

The troop probably has one or more assistant Scoutmasters. They support the Scoutmaster and carry some of the troop's adult leadership load. An assistant Scoutmaster may be assigned a specific responsibility such as working with a new-Scout patrol or a Venture patrol.

—*The Scoutmaster Handbook*

A great reward for a Scoutmaster is in helping a young man who has accepted a position of responsibility in a Scout troop develop into a senior patrol leader capable of fulfilling the high expectations placed upon him. For a Scout, serving as senior patrol leader is a chance to work closely with an adult willing to provide vision, guidance, and encouragement.

The Troop Committee

The troop committee may be seen as a board of directors. Troop committees are often composed of Scouts' parents and members of the troop's chartered organization who are interested in youth programs. In support of the troop's program and administrative matters, committee members play a role in:

- Selecting adult leaders for the troop.
- Developing community service projects.
- Arranging transportation for outings.
- Planning and assisting in fund-raising.
- Providing for special needs and assistance for individual Scouts.
- Serving on boards of review and at courts of honor.
- Helping troop leaders maintain financial and advancement records.
- Maintaining adequate outdoor equipment.

The Chartered Organization Representative

Every Scout troop is part of the youth program of a service club, religious institution, or other community organization that has been granted a charter by the Boy Scouts of America. The charter permits the organization to conduct the Scouting program in accordance with its own policies and guidelines as well as those of the BSA.

A chartered organization representative serves as a link between the organization and the Scout unit. A chartered institution may also sponsor a Cub Scout pack, a Varsity team, and a Venturing crew—all of them served by the same chartered organization representative.

Understanding the Troop's Structure

In addition to the troop's adult leaders, you will be able to rely on the youth leaders of the troop. Depending on the size and needs of the troop, these may include an assistant senior patrol leader, junior assistant Scoutmasters, troop guides, the leader of each patrol, and Scouts serving as the troop's quartermaster, scribe, historian, librarian, instructors, and chaplain aide.

Patrols serve as the building blocks of a troop. The patrol leaders and other troop leaders who make up the patrol leaders' council are deeply involved in planning the troop's program and in carrying out monthly meetings and activities. As a result, an effective troop has a program that is run by the Scouts themselves, is of the greatest interest to the most troop members, and provides many opportunities for Scouts to sharpen their leadership skills.

Sample Youth Leader Organizational Chart for a Large Troop

In this sample, there are enough members to fill all of the patrols and leadership positions.

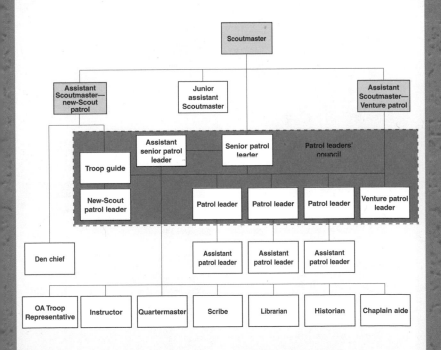

Sample Youth Leader Organizational Chart for a Small Troop

As more boys join, more patrols can be formed and more leadership positions filled.

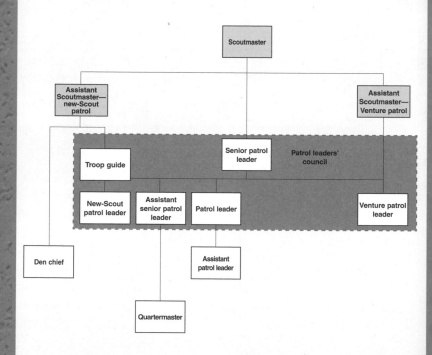

Your Leadership Training Opportunities

Leadership training provided by the BSA will help you get off on the right foot as senior patrol leader. As you gain leadership experience, additional training opportunities can assist you in increasing your effectiveness and confidence.

Introduction to Leadership

Soon after you become senior patrol leader, the Scoutmaster will schedule an introductory meeting with you. The session may include a small group of other troop leaders and probably will last about an hour. No doubt the Scoutmaster will express pleasure in having you serve as senior patrol leader and will remind you how important your contribution to the troop will be.

The discussion you have with the Scoutmaster may also cover specific leadership suggestions for upcoming troop meetings and activities. Expect to learn about ways the troop's adult leaders will support you and provide guidance, and where you can find other BSA resources of value to senior patrol leaders.

The Senior Patrol Leader Handbook **you are holding is one of the most useful leadership tools available to you.** *The Boy Scout Handbook, Fieldbook,* **and other Scouting manuals can also be of great assistance.**

Troop Leadership Training

The Troop Leadership Training workshop will be held soon after your election and will involve all the troop's youth leaders. It consists of three hourlong modules that cover the basics of what a youth leader must Be, what he must Know, and what he must Do. It is designed to answer three basic questions:

- What is my role?
- What does success look like in my role?
- What is expected of me?

The objective of Troop Leadership Training is to give you a clearer picture of how your position fits in the troop and how you can make a difference.

National Youth Leadership Training, National Leadership Seminars, and National Advanced Youth Leadership Experience

You may be invited to attend a weeklong National Youth Leadership Training conference offered by the local council. It will introduce you to more advanced leadership skills. Additional youth leadership training opportunities are offered through the Order of the Arrow and Philmont Training Center. They are designed to strengthen your knowledge and application of leadership skills in your troop. They will enhance your ability to serve others and make your troop successful.

A leadership experience can be frustrating and disappointing without adequate training. The best source of training is to attend a weeklong training experience.

How Will I Know I Am Leading Well?

As senior patrol leader, you will be faced with a broad variety of leadership situations. Much of the time, the troop will experience terrific successes as the plans of the patrol leaders' council unfold in rich and rewarding ways. Now and then, though, the troop will be confronted by activities and events that bear little resemblance to what you had imagined. It is all part of the Scouting experience.

Through good times and bad, the first clue that you are leading well is that you are doing your best. You are using the knowledge you have and the resources around you to help the troop find a way through any situation. By staying cheerful and by always looking for solutions to problems confronting the troop members, you will set an example for others. That sort of leadership can help a group rise up to meet the toughest challenges.

For immediate feedback, get together with the patrol leaders' council at the end of each meeting or troop activity and take a few minutes to talk about recent events. You can learn a great deal by reflecting on some or all of the following questions:

- In what ways did things go as expected? In what ways did they not?

- How good was our planning and preparation? What could we have done better?

- What did troop members like best about this experience? What would they change next time?

- What did we learn during this event?

- As we prepare for future events, what are some of the ways we can make our troop even better?

The Scoutmaster also can offer supportive evaluation of your leadership efforts. By sharing with the Scoutmaster your thoughts about a just-concluded event or meeting, you often will find that you can better prepare yourself to lead upcoming troop activities.

Leadership Tips to Get You Started

There are lots of ways to be a good senior patrol leader. Over time, you will learn many of them. The adult leaders of the troop and the other members of the patrol leaders' council will help you put effective leadership methods into practice. On your own, you will also figure out much about leading through trial and error.

All of that will take time, of course. The following tips can help you lead the troop right from the start. You may already have used some of them when you were a patrol leader or while you held other offices in the troop. These tips can prove effective in nearly every setting where you are called upon to be a leader:

- **Keep your word.** Don't make promises you can't keep.

- **Be fair to all.** A good leader shows no favorites. Don't allow friendships to stand in the way of treating all members of the troop equally. Get to know the interests of troop members and try to assign responsibilities to Scouts according to their strengths.

- **Communicate.** A good leader knows how to get and give information so that everyone understands. You do not need a commanding voice, but you do need to be a good listener. Understanding what the members of the patrol are thinking will help you guide them in the right direction.

- **Be flexible.** Meetings, campouts, and other patrol events will not always go as planned. Be open to new opportunities, and be willing to shift to a different plan if original expectations change.

- **Be organized.** Time spent preparing for troop meetings and events will be repaid many times over. Ensure that the troop scribe keeps accurate notes of the decisions and assignments made by the patrol leaders' council. Checklists and meeting agendas can be invaluable organizational aids.

- **Delegate.** Among the greatest strengths of a good leader is the willingness to empower others to accomplish all they can. Most people like to be challenged. They want to be trusted to carry their share of the load. Encourage troop members to do things they can do well and to increase their knowledge and confidence by taking on tasks they have never tried.

- **Set the example.** Whatever you do, Scouts in the troop are likely to do the same. Lead by example, both while you are in uniform and throughout other parts of your life.

- **Be consistent.** Nothing is more confusing for a group than a leader who is one way one moment and the opposite a short time later. When the troop members know what to expect from you, they will be more likely to respond positively to your leadership.

- **Give praise.** Offer honest compliments whenever you can. A simple "Nice job!" can go a long way toward making a Scout feel he is contributing to the advancement of the troop.

- **Ask for help.** Do not be embarrassed to draw on the many resources available to you. When confronted with a situation you do not know how to handle—or just to get another opinion on a plan that seems to be going well—ask experienced troop leaders for guidance and advice.

- **Criticize in private.** There will be times when you must provide a Scout with critical feedback. Pull the Scout aside and quietly explain what he is doing wrong. Add a suggestion on how it should be done correctly.

- **Have fun.** Most of all, have fun learning to be a leader. Your joy and enthusiasm will spread to other Scouts and will help energize the activities of the troop.

Name _____

What does success look like for our troop? _____

_____

_____

_____

_____

_____

_____

_____

_____

What are my goals to get us there? _____

_____

_____

_____

_____

_____

_____

_____

_____

_____

_____

Your Troop

Scoutmaster

Address

E-mail

Telephone

Senior patrol leader

Address

E-mail

Telephone

Troop guide

Address

E-mail

Telephone

Assistant Scoutmaster

Address

E-mail

Telephone

Assistant Scoutmaster

Address

E-mail

Telephone

Assistant senior patrol leader

Address

E-mail

Telephone

Patrol leader

Address

E-mail

Telephone

Patrol leader

Address

E-mail

Telephone

Patrol leader

Address

E-mail

Telephone

Quartermaster

Address

E-mail

Telephone

Scribe

Address

E-mail

Telephone

Historian

Address

E-mail

Telephone

Librarian

Address

E-mail

Telephone

Chaplain aide

Address

E-mail

Telephone

2 Building Troop Spirit

Building Troop Spirit

Spirit is an important concept in

Scouting, both for individuals and for groups of Scouts. Scout spirit, patrol spirit, and troop spirit can energize the program of the Boy Scouts of America and bring the fullest meaning to the Scouting experience.

- *Scout spirit* means that you live by the Scout Oath and Law, are prepared for anything that comes along, and are willing to give time and energy to do service for someone in need in the community. Showing Scout spirit is a requirement for all the ranks of Boy Scouting.

- *Patrol spirit* puts the spotlight on the Scouts who have formed together as a patrol. They demonstrate patrol spirit by working toward the common goal of building the best possible patrol. They move ahead as a team, achieving more as a team than they could as individuals.

- *Troop spirit* focuses on the unity, enthusiasm, and progress of the entire troop.

As senior patrol leader, you can help the troop recognize the importance of troop spirit and guide everyone in taking full advantage of Scouting's opportunities. Among the most effective means you have for building troop spirit are the methods of Scouting.

The Methods of Scouting

The Boy Scouts of America uses eight fundamental methods to meet its members' expectations for fun and adventure and to achieve Scouting's aims of encouraging character development, citizenship, and mental and physical fitness. A Scout troop functions best when all eight methods are employed.

The Methods of Scouting

1. The ideals
2. The patrol method
3. The outdoors
4. Advancement
5. Association with adults
6. Personal growth
7. Leadership development
8. The uniform

Method 1—The Ideals

The ideals of the Boy Scouts of America are spelled out in the Scout Oath, Scout Law, Scout motto, and Scout slogan. Scout meetings, outdoor adventures, and other Scout activities reinforce these ideals.

Method 2—The Patrol Method

Made up of Scouts of similar ages and experience levels, the patrols of a troop help their members develop a sense of pride and identity. The patrol members elect their leader, divide the tasks to be done, and share in the satisfaction of accepting and fulfilling group responsibilities.

Each patrol expresses its patrol spirit with a patrol name, flag, yell, and song. Members of a patrol may also master a specialty—orienteering, for example, or Dutch oven cooking—and use it as their trademark.

National Honor Patrol Award

Encourage all of the patrols in the troop to work toward earning the National Honor Patrol Award. Here are the requirements:

- Have a patrol name, flag, and yell. Put the patrol design on equipment, and use the patrol yell. Keep patrol records up-to-date.

- Hold two patrol meetings every month.

- Take part in at least one hike, outdoor activity, or other Scouting event.

- Complete two Good Turns or service projects approved by the patrol leaders' council.

- Help two patrol members advance one rank.

- Note that at least 75 percent of patrol members wear the full uniform correctly.

- Have a representative attend at least three patrol leaders' council meetings.

- Have eight members in the patrol, or increase patrol membership over the previous three-months.

Method 3—The Outdoors

Much of the Scouting program is designed to take place outdoors in settings where Scouts can find real adventure. Outdoor activities help put sizzle into Scouting and keep troop members coming back for more. A troop with a strong outdoor program is well on its way to finding success in all areas.

A Note on Patrol Outdoor Activities

Most patrol activities take place within the framework of the troop. However, patrols also may set out on day hikes, service projects, and overnighters independent of the troop and free of adult leadership as long as they follow two rules:

- The Scoutmaster must approve the patrol activity.
- The patrol activity cannot interfere with any troop function.

A patrol activity without adult supervision should be allowed only when it has been thoroughly planned and the Scoutmaster is satisfied the activity is well within patrol members' levels of training and responsibility. If the Scoutmaster has any doubts, he should encourage the patrol to reconsider its plans or assign adults to accompany the patrol during the activity.
The Scoutmaster Handbook

Method 4—Advancement

The Boy Scouts of America believes that a Scout should receive recognition for his achievements. The requirements for the ranks of Tenderfoot through First Class prepare boys to take full advantage of all that Scouting has to offer. Earning merit badges allows them to explore many fields, helps them round out their skills, and perhaps introduces them to subjects that will become lifelong interests and rewarding careers.

As one of the eight methods of Scouting, advancement is a natural outgrowth of the other seven. A boy whose Scouting experience is introducing him to BSA ideals, the patrol method, the outdoors, association with adults, personal growth, leadership development, and the uniform will almost certainly find himself moving steadily along the BSA's advancement trail.

Method 5—Association With Adults

Scouts learn a great deal by watching how older troop members conduct themselves. A senior patrol leader who is willing to listen and encourage can make a profound difference in the lives of others, especially a troop's youngest Scouts.

Method 6—Personal Growth

Youth of Boy Scout age are experiencing dramatic physical and emotional growth. Scouting offers them opportunities to channel much of that change into productive endeavors and to find the answers they are seeking for many of their questions. Through service projects and Good Turns, Scouts can discover their place in their community. Religious award programs offer pathways for them to more deeply understand their place in the world. The troop itself provides each Scout with an arena in which to explore, to try out new ideas, and sometimes simply to embark on adventures with no design other than the joy of having a good time with good people.

Method 7—Leadership Development

Leadership is a skill that can be learned only by practice. Every Scout in a patrol and troop will find over time that he is filling leadership positions of increasing responsibility. Serving as patrol leader and as senior patrol leader can give Scouts the confidence and ability to be leaders in the future.

Method 8—The Uniform

Since 1910, the Boy Scout uniform has been a recognizable part of the American scene. Wearing the uniform helps boys develop a sense of belonging to their troop. It reinforces the fact that all members of the BSA are equals.

People seeing a boy in a Scout uniform expect someone of good character who is prepared to the best of his ability to help those around him. Likewise, the senior patrol leader in uniform sets a good example for everyone in the troop.

Troop Traditions

As senior patrol leader, you can encourage each patrol to establish an identity of its own. Strong patrol spirit leads, in turn, to troop spirit. Work with patrol leaders to ensure that every patrol has a patrol name, flag, yell, and song. Guide them toward developing specialties of their own, too.

In much the same way that patrols develop patrol spirit, a troop can build on its traditions to enhance its identity. It can also develop new traditions for the future.

Troop Flag

A BSA flag with the troop's number can be presented by a color guard at the openings of meetings. It may fly over troop campsites and lead the way for the troop when Scouts are taking part in camporees, summer camps, and other Scouting activities. Ribbons and similar awards won by the troop can be secured to the flag-pole for all to see.

Troop Yell

Perhaps you have seen members of a troop at a camporee hiking into camp chanting their troop yell. It was a unique way for them to announce their arrival and to share in the spirit of the event. A troop yell can be a chant related to the troop's number and hometown. It might include the names of the patrols making up the troop.

Troop Uniform

The Scout uniform can be a source of troop pride and spirit. Many troops have a special neckerchief worn by members, or a hat of a certain color and style. A troop's activity uniform may include a T-shirt emblazoned with the troop's emblem or some other significant reminder of the troop's identity.

Recruiting New Members

Scouting has much to offer young people. Likewise, new members bring fresh energy and ideas to Scouting, keeping it strong and vital. Scouts who enjoy a troop's program will want their friends to join, too. Cub Scouts seeing Boy Scouts setting out on adventures and learning outdoor skills will look forward to the time when they can join a troop and take off for the backcountry, too.

The best way for a troop to increase its membership is to have an exciting program that boys want to enjoy. You have a hand in that by being a good senior patrol leader. You can also help by telling other boys about the troop and its program and by inviting them to come to a troop meeting and see what Scouting has to offer.

Look for more formal opportunities to share information about Scouting, too. In many communities, the week of the BSA's anniversary can be a chance for you to talk about the troop at school assemblies and gatherings of community organizations and church groups. If you have them, bring along scrapbooks and photo albums showing the troop in action. You may be pleasantly surprised to discover how many people become interested in Scouting because of the example set by you and the other Scouts in the troop.

3 The Troop Program

The Troop Program

You would not think of setting out

on a long backpacking trip without having a map to show you the way. The same is true of the troop's program—the plan you develop is an essential map that shows where the troop is headed, where the challenges lie, and the exciting opportunities that Scouts can expect to find along the way.

While you may be new to the role of senior patrol leader, you probably have been around Scouting long enough to have a good idea what needs to be done in the coming months. If the patrol leaders' council has already planned the troop's program, you should have a clear sense of the direction the troop will go. Much of your work will be in seeing that the program plan comes to life.

You also will be involved in determining the contents of the troop's program. One of your first responsibilities as senior patrol leader will be to combine your energies with those of the Scoutmaster to put together a program planning conference for the patrol leaders' council and to assist them in developing a program plan—a map to guide the troop.

The Long and Short of Program Planning

Troop program planning has two phases: long-term and short-term.

- *Long-term planning* occurs at the annual troop program planning conference. You will be helping the patrol leaders' council and the Scoutmaster determine what the troop will be doing for the next 12 months.

- *Short-term planning* happens during monthly meetings of the patrol leaders' council. By reviewing the annual program plan and filling in the details, troop leaders can finalize details of the troop's meetings and activities for the coming four weeks.

The Annual Troop Program Planning Conference

The troop program planning conference offers the patrol leaders' council the opportunity to draw up an effective, exciting course of action. The conference is organized and conducted by the senior patrol leader with the help of the Scoutmaster.

There is no set time of the year to conduct the conference, though many troops prefer late summer after the troop has returned from summer camp. Set the date well in advance so that all members of the patrol leaders' council can clear their schedules to attend. The conference should be in a setting that is free of distractions—a remote cabin or campsite can be ideal. The essential business of the conference usually can be conducted in one day, though the workload can be spread out over two days with an evening of camping in between. The pace of the conference should be relaxed and informal.

Preparing for and conducting a troop program planning conference involves a five-step process:

1. Do your homework.

2. Get patrol input.

3. Hold the planning conference.

4. Consult with the troop committee.

5. Announce the plan.

Program Features

The BSA offers a wealth of exciting program features that can serve as a guide in planning a troop program. There are 36 program features offered in *Troop Program Features, Volumes I, II,* and *III.* Each program feature provides advancement opportunities, troop meeting outlines, and an outdoor event to top off the program feature.

Troop Program Features, Volume I, No. 33110

Troop Program Features, Volume II, No. 33111

Troop Program Features, Volume III, No. 33112

The program features are:

Aquatics	Environment	Physical fitness
Athletics	First aid	Pioneering
Backpacking	Fishing	Public service
Boating/canoeing	Forestry	Safety
Business	Health care	Science
Camping	High adventure	Shooting
Citizenship	Hiking	Special cooking
Communications	Hobbies	Sports
Cooking	Leadership	Tracking
Cultural awareness	Mechanics	Wilderness survival
Emergency preparedness	Nature	Wildlife management
Engineering	Orienteering	Winter camping

Step 1: Do Your Homework

This step should be done jointly by you and the Scoutmaster well in advance of the planning conference:

1. Evaluate the troop's past year.

2. Review the video *Troop Program Planning*, No. AV-02V010.

3. Gather district and council dates such as camporees and summer camp.

4. Gather dates of community functions, key school events and activities, holidays, and special events of the chartered organization.

5. Review the advancement status of the troop members and decide what kinds of activities are needed to help each boy progress.

6. Write down the priorities you feel are most important for the troop. These could include summer camp, high-adventure activities, advancement goals, the Quality Unit Award, service projects, and fund-raising events.

Step 2: Get Patrol Input

At a monthly patrol leaders' council meeting, present the list of priorities you and the Scoutmaster have developed and explore the range of options you believe are available to the troop. For example, you might feel that the needs of the troop can be best achieved by adopting any of 36 selected program features available from the BSA publications *Troop Program Features, Volumes I, II,* and *III,* Nos. 33110, 33111, and 33112.

Paring down those possibilities to a dozen—one for each month—will be easier to do after patrol leaders have shared the list with patrol members and gotten their thoughts on the features that most interest them. Remind patrol leaders to bring their patrols' recommendations to the program planning conference.

Step 3: Hold the Troop Program Planning Conference

The troop's planning conference is an opportunity for members of the patrol leaders' council to map out the troop's activities for the year and for the troop's adult leaders to offer guidance and support. In consultation with the Scoutmaster, set a time and a place for the conference and invite the following persons to attend:

In an active role:

- Senior patrol leader
- Assistant senior patrol leader
- All patrol leaders
- Troop guide

In a supportive role:

- Scoutmaster
- Assistant Scoutmasters
- Junior assistant Scoutmasters

The troop scribe may be invited to the conference to keep a log of the proceedings. However, he is not a voting member of the conference.

During the program planning process, patrol leaders are speaking for all the members of their patrols rather than expressing their own personal preferences. Likewise, you as senior patrol leader should do all you can to represent the wishes of everyone in the troop.

Open the conference with a team-building activity or an action game that will promote cooperation among the participants. Showing part two of the video *Troop Program Planning* can set the stage for the conference as it reminds those in attendance of the importance of the work they are about to do.

ANNUAL TROOP PROGRAM PLANNING CONFERENCE AGENDA

The intent of the annual troop program planning conference is fourfold:

- Develop troop goals for the coming year.
- Select the major events for the coming year.
- Select the program features for the coming year.
- Fill out the troop's calendar for the coming year.

Develop Troop Goals

The Scoutmaster leads a discussion that guides the group in developing a list of the goals they want to see the troop achieve in the next 12 months. The Scoutmaster may present a list of goals and then encourage the group to expand upon them or adjust the list to better fit the needs of troop members.

By majority vote the patrol leaders' council approves the troop goals.

Select the Major Events

With the Scoutmaster's assistance, you as senior patrol leader review potential major events for the troop—summer camp, Scout shows, etc. These events may be entered on a calendar and photo-copied for everyone's information.

Invite patrol leaders to share input resulting from the patrols' discussions of the proposed major events for the troop. Be sure to consider the preparation time required for each event and how that will affect the troop's calendar.

Open the floor for discussion of any or all of the proposed events. Encourage input from every conference participant.

Decide by a majority vote whether to include each major event on the troop's annual calendar. Enter the elected items on the Troop Planning Work Sheet, from *Troop Program Features*.

Conference Materials

You and the Scoutmaster can find a detailed agenda for an annual troop planning conference in the BSA publication *Troop Program Resources*. The agenda will guide you through much of the planning for the conference and offer guidance for managing the conference itself. Have copies of essential worksheets on hand for those attending the conference. *Troop Program Resources* also lists other confer-ence materials you may find useful. The Scoutmaster can help ensure that these are made available.

Select the Program Features

With the Scoutmaster's help, the senior patrol leader presents the list of potential monthly program features.

Open the floor to discuss each of the program features. Consider the following questions:

- Will the program feature help the troop meet its goals?
- What opportunities for advancement does it present?
- Where would the feature best fit into the annual calendar?

    Vote on the list of program features.

Fill Out the Troop's Calendar

Using the Troop Planning Work Sheet, develop the troop's calendar by writing the following items in their appropriate spots:

- Monthly program features
- Boards of review
- Courts of honor
- Recruitment nights
- Webelos Scout graduation
- Any other troop activities that can be scheduled this far in advance
- Service project for the chartered organization

Lead the group in a review of the Troop Planning Work Sheet. Once the group has approved the final edition of the plan, it will be ready to present to the troop committee for its input and approval.

Plan the troop program for the upcoming month, beginning by showing part three of the *Troop Program Planning* video.

Close the troop's annual program planning conference by inviting the Scoutmaster to offer a Scoutmaster's Minute.

Step 4: Consult With the Troop Committee and the Chartered Organization

The senior patrol leader and the Scoutmaster should present the plan to the troop committee and the chartered organization representative and ask for their support. If revisions are suggested, the senior patrol leader must take the plan back to the patrol leaders' council for changes to be made and approved.

Step 5: Announce the Plan

Distribute copies of the final plan to troop members, parents and guardians of Scouts, members of the troop committee, and representatives of the chartered organization. Copies of the plan also should be given to the Cub Scout pack leaders, unit commissioners, the district executive, the head and secretary of the chartered organization, and the building custodian.

The Monthly Patrol Leaders' Council Meeting

The patrol leaders' council runs the troop according to the policies of the Boy Scouts of America under the guidance and counsel of the Scoutmaster. The patrol leaders' council plans the troop program at the annual program planning conference. It then meets every four weeks to fine-tune the plans for the coming month.

Planning Repays Itself Many Times Over

Plan out the details of each activity, list the steps required to make it happen, and assign responsibilities to members of the patrol leaders' council.

At the conclusion of troop meetings (and at other times the senior patrol leader feels the patrol leaders' council should consider an issue) the council meets informally (a "stand-up meeting") to review the success of a troop activity and to go over responsibilities for future meetings and events.

The Scoutmaster is present at patrol leaders' council meetings, but only in a supportive role to provide information and insight on issues and activities. To the greatest extent possible, it is the members of the patrol leaders' council who plan and carry out the program of a boy-run, boy-led troop.

In addition to program planning, the patrol leaders' council may deal with other issues concerning the troop and its members:

- Advancement needs
- Special ceremonies and awards
- Fund-raising projects
- Good Turn programs
- Conservation projects
- Special programs with the chartered organization
- Scout Sunday, Sabbath, and Scouting Anniversary Week
- Recruitment plans
- Webelos graduation
- Special ceremonies
- Community events such as parades and festivals
- Disciplinary issues

Patrol leaders' council meetings can be held in any private place free of distractions. The best setting will allow everyone to face each other and have adequate space in which to work. The length of each meeting will vary from 60 to 90 minutes depending on the amount of business before the council.

As senior patrol leader, you will chair meetings of the patrol leaders' council. Stick to the agenda and keep things moving along. If council members are spending too much time on an issue, it may be necessary to table that item for future consideration and move on with the agenda. Keep the council focused on issues of importance.

A Boy Scout troop should be boy-run and boy-led. Scouts plan the program they want and then make it come to life.

To a large extent, the Scoutmaster serves a troop as a coach, mentor, and resource for the senior patrol leader and other youth leaders. The Scoutmaster also has the authority and obligation to step in whenever a Scouting event or activity may violate BSA policy or could jeopardize anyone's safety or well-being. In those situations, a Scoutmaster can recommend an alternative plan that does fall within BSA guidelines.

Patrol Leaders' Council Meeting Agenda

Activity	Run by
Opening and Call to Order	Senior Patrol Leader
Roll Call and Reading of the Log (Minutes)	Troop Scribe
Patrol Reports	Patrol Leaders
Old Business	Senior Patrol Leader
Big Event Planning	Senior Patrol Leader
Troop Meeting Planning	Senior Patrol Leader
New Business	Senior Patrol Leader
Scoutmaster's Minute	Scoutmaster

The Parts of a Patrol Leaders' Council Meeting

OPENING AND CALL TO ORDER

Start the meeting on time with a simple opening ceremony such as reciting the Scout Oath or Pledge of Allegiance.

ROLL CALL AND READING OF THE LOG

Ask the troop scribe to call the roll and read the log from the previous meeting. Council members may make additions or corrections to the log before voting to approve it as part of the council's permanent record.

PATROL REPORTS

Each patrol leader should be prepared to make a report on the progress of his patrol. His report should include information about new members, advancement progress, and anything the patrol has done since the last patrol leaders' council meeting.

OLD BUSINESS

Take up any discussion items left unresolved at the last patrol leaders' council meeting. When necessary, bring matters to a close by asking for a vote.

BIG EVENT PLANNING

Review and discuss the big event related to the upcoming month's troop program feature. While the event itself will have already been determined during the troop program planning conference, details may need to be worked out. Determine the who, what, where, when, why, and how of the event. Patrol leaders can add to the discussion by voicing ideas raised by their patrols. Explore the issues and bring any essential matters to a vote.

TROOP MEETING PLANNING

Distribute Troop Meeting Plan Work Sheets for each of the month's troop meetings. (The plan sheets can be found in the BSA publication *Troop Program Features*.) As you and the patrol leaders' council review plans for each of the month's four meetings, assign responsibilities for portions of the meetings, taking care to distribute the load equally among the patrols and troop leaders. Be sure to plan three levels of skills instruction for each meeting so that all age groups will be equally challenged.

NEW BUSINESS

This portion of the meeting is devoted to discussions of items not previously on the agenda. A patrol may be requesting permission to embark on a patrol hike, for example, or the opportunity for a special troop service project may have recently come up.

Among the issues to be addressed by the patrol leaders' council are any disciplinary problems within the troop. The troop's youth leaders can consider the best ways to encourage appropriate behavior by each Scout and develop strategies for dealing with

Members of the Patrol Leaders' Council

The patrol leaders' council is made up of the following people:

- Senior patrol leader
- Assistant senior patrol leader
- Patrol leaders of each patrol, including the new-Scout patrol and the Venture patrol (If a patrol leader cannot attend, the assistant patrol leader should represent the patrol in his absence.)
- Troop guide

The troop scribe may attend to take minutes but is not a voting member of the council.

any instances of inappropriate behavior. Information about more serious behavior problems should be passed on to the Scoutmaster and troop committee so that they can handle the situation, often by meeting with the Scout and his parents or guardians.

SCOUTMASTER'S MINUTE

Up to now the Scoutmaster probably observed the patrol leaders' council meeting and asked a question or two, but otherwise allowed you to run the meeting and guide the agenda. As a closing to the meeting, the Scoutmaster can share some constructive thoughts on what has happened and offer an upbeat, supportive Scoutmaster's Minute to provide a sense of completion to the proceedings.

Assessing the Patrol Leaders' Council Meeting

Immediately following a meeting of the patrol leaders' council, take a few minutes to review events with the Scoutmaster. The following questions can guide your assessment:

- Was there a written agenda, and was it followed?
- Were all patrols allowed input on troop decisions?
- Were specific tasks assigned to individuals?
- Were necessary resources for troop activities considered?
- Were the tasks spread evenly among patrols and individuals?
- Was a specific schedule planned for upcoming events?
- Did the group come to a consensus on handling problems?
- Was a log kept?

Follow-up Makes It Happen

At the conclusion of an effective patrol leaders' council meeting, the troop's youth leaders should understand the plan for troop meetings and events. They also will understand who is responsible for various portions of those meetings and events and be clear about what information must be shared with the patrols.

In the weeks to come, check in with patrol leaders' council members now and then to ensure that they continue to be on top of the troop's plans. Get them together before and after meetings and activities to double-check their understanding of the manner in which events will unfold and to review the just-concluded troop events.

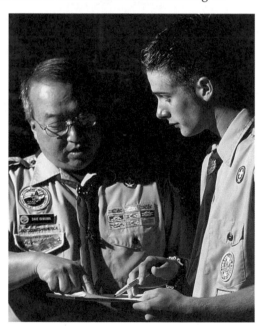

You and the Scoutmaster will also visit briefly before meetings and activities to look over the agenda developed by the patrol leaders' council and ensure that everything is ready to go according to plan.

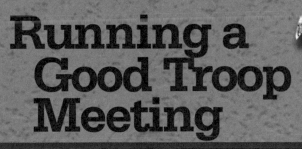

Running a Good Troop Meeting

4

Running a Good Troop Meeting

The weekly meeting is the glue that holds a Scout troop together. Well-planned meetings run by the troop's youth leaders can be full of excitement and satisfaction. Meeting time devoted to learning new skills and organizing future campouts, service projects, and other activities will help keep interest levels and enthusiasm high.

Troop meetings serve many purposes, including these:

- **Motivating Scouts.** From Scouts' points of view, troop meetings are chances for them to get together with their friends for fun and adventure. For Scoutmasters, meetings offer many avenues to encourage Scouts to learn, to advance, and to improve themselves.

- **Strengthening patrols.** Patrols have opportunities at troop meetings to meet together, to learn as a team, and to share what they know. Whether they serve as the honor guard during an opening flag ceremony, as the presenters of a Scouting skill, or as the organizers of a game or activity, every patrol can contribute to every troop meeting.

- **Learning and practicing Scouting skills.** A portion of a troop meeting may be devoted to the demonstration and practice of skills that will enhance Scouts' ability to hike and camp, and to pass requirements for higher ranks.

- **Exercising leadership.** The troop's youth leaders take leading roles in planning, conducting, and assessing the success of troop meetings. Leadership is a skill that can be learned only by experience, and troop meetings serve as regular occasions for that to happen.

- **Promoting Scout spirit.** Troop meetings offer ideal settings for patrols to take part in contests and competitions that test their expertise and their abilities to cooperate with one another.

Most troops have a troop meeting or an activity every week. Meetings should occur at the same time every week to help boys and their families schedule effectively. If a troop has camped all weekend, the patrol leaders' council may decide to forego the meeting the following week. Most troop meetings occur on week-nights and should not last longer than 90 minutes to get boys home in time for homework and adequate rest. Troop meetings should not always be held at the same place. For example, now and then a troop may meet at a fire station or police headquarters so the members can learn about how their town is protected. On a summer evening, they might gather at a local pool to pass some of the swimming requirements for a rank or merit badge.

Weekly troop meetings should be fun and full of action and excitement. They can be opportunities to learn new skills and plan future activities and service projects. Aside from the Scoutmaster's

Minute, the content and conduct of each section of a troop meeting is the responsibility of the Scouts themselves.

Planning a Troop Meeting

Responsibility for the conduct and content of a troop meeting falls to the Scouts themselves. Troop meetings are planned well in advance by the senior patrol leader and the patrol leaders' council.

Each troop meeting should have been planned the previous month at the meeting of the patrol leaders' council. The senior patrol leader will have assigned patrols and individuals to take care of portions of a meeting, giving as many Scouts as possible the chance to contribute. The seven-part troop meeting plan provides the framework for efficient, well-run troop meetings.

The Seven Parts of a Troop Meeting

1. Preopening

2. Opening

3. Skills instruction

4. Patrol meetings

5. Interpatrol activity

6. Closing—Scoutmaster's Minute

7. After the meeting

TROOP MEETING PLAN

Date _____

ACTIVITY	DESCRIPTION	RUN BY	TIME
Preopening _____ minutes			
Opening Ceremony _____ minutes			
Skills Instruction _____ minutes			
Patrol Meetings _____ minutes			
Interpatrol Activity _____ minutes			
Closing _____ minutes Total 90 minutes of meeting	• Scoutmaster's Minute.	SM	
After the Meeting			

Using the Troop Meeting Plan

The seven-part plan for troop meetings is an important guide, but use it flexibly. The times noted in the plan are suggestions only and can vary to fit various situations. For example, the troop may be getting ready for a campout. The usual amount of time set aside for patrol meetings might be expanded to allow Scouts time to complete their patrol camping preparations. A troop nearing the date of a district camporee may devote extra time to skills instruction so that everyone will be ready for activities involving the theme of the camporee, and the interpatrol activity can include an extended competition that also focuses on the key skills.

When the minutes allotted to one part of the troop meeting plan increase, consider shortening other portions of the plan. Every troop meeting should be interesting and useful, and it should begin and end on time.

THE PREOPENING

As Scouts begin to arrive for a troop meeting, a patrol leader or an older Scout assigned by the senior patrol leader should get them involved in a preopening game or project designed so that additional Scouts can join as they show up. The preopening is often well suited for the outdoors. Those in charge of the preopening activity should be ready to start about 15 minutes before the scheduled beginning of the meeting. Varying the activities from week to week will keep the preopening fresh.

Scouts whose patrol has been assigned to serve that week as the *service patrol* should use the preopening time to prepare for the troop meeting. The meeting room may need to be rearranged, chairs set up, flags displayed, and other preparations completed before the meeting can begin.

THE OPENING (5 MINUTES)

Call the meeting to order on time, instructing Scouts to line up in formation by patrol. The patrol responsible for the opening ceremony may conduct a flag ceremony and then lead the troop members in the Scout Oath and Law and the Pledge of Allegiance.

SKILLS INSTRUCTION (15 TO 20 MINUTES)

This portion of the meeting is devoted to the mastery of knowledge that Scouts need to participate fully in an upcoming activity, or upon skills they must learn to complete advancement requirements.

The skills to be taught at each meeting will have been determined in advance by the patrol leaders' council. Often the skills will relate directly to the month's program plan for troop activities. Instruction should be hands-on learning rather than lecturing. All skill instruction should follow a simple process called the Teaching EDGE. First, the skill is explained, then demonstrated. Then the learner is guided as he tries the skill. Enabling, the last E in EDGE, means creating an environment for the trainee to continue to be successful (like providing an opportunity to practice and use the skill).

Those who may be effective in teaching skills are the troop guide, instructors, junior assistant Scoutmasters, assistant Scoutmasters, and members of the troop committee. Older Scouts and members of the Venture patrol also can be effective instructors, though at most meetings they will be involved in their own activities.

Whenever possible, troop skills instruction should be divided into three levels:

❶ Basic Scouting skills instruction for the new Scouts

❷ Advanced instruction for the experienced Scouts

❸ Expert instruction for the Venture patrol

Each instructional area should be separated from the others so there are no distractions.

The Scoutmaster probably has a good idea of who has skills to teach. By using the Troop Resource Survey, No. 34437, a troop's Scoutmaster can identify other ways Scouting leaders and parents can assist with the troop's program.

PATROL MEETINGS (5 TO 20 MINUTES)

End skills instruction on time and ask patrols to go to their patrol areas for their patrol meeting. Patrol leaders will take charge of the patrols.

Matters to be dealt with during a patrol meeting include taking attendance, collecting dues, planning the patrol's involvement in upcoming troop activities, selecting menus for hikes and campouts, assigning patrol members to specific tasks, and working out any other details for the smooth operation of the patrol.

Circulate among the patrol meetings and be ready to serve as a resource if a patrol leader asks for your assistance. If you notice that patrols have completed their work, call the patrols back together and move on to the next part of the troop meeting.

INTERPATROL ACTIVITY (15 TO 20 MINUTES)

You or someone appointed by you can lead this opportunity for the patrols to interact with one another in a competitive or a cooperative effort. The activity might be a game that will test the skills the Scouts are learning for an upcoming activity—pitching tents or tying knots, for example. *Troop Program Resources* has a wealth of games that foster friendly teamwork and competition. The BSA manual *Project COPE,* No. 34371, also contains many appropriate games and challenges.

CLOSING—SCOUTMASTER'S MINUTE (5 MINUTES)

The closing of a meeting is the Scoutmaster's opportunity to step forward. Ask everyone to sit quietly, then turn the meeting over to the Scoutmaster for reminders and announcements about upcoming events, and support of the patrols for their achievements and progress.

The highlight of the closing will be the Scoutmaster's Minute, a brief message built on one of Scouting's values. As the concluding thought of a troop meeting, the Scoutmaster's Minute is a message each person can carry home.

THE "AFTER THE MEETING" MEETING (5 MINUTES)

Ask members of the patrol leaders' council to stay a few moments after the closing to discuss with you and the Scoutmaster the quality of the just-concluded meeting. Offer praise for portions of the meeting that went well, and talk about ways that future troop meetings can be improved. Make a few written notes so that suggestions can be explored more fully at the next patrol leaders' council meeting.

Here are some questions to ask:

- What should we start doing that would make the meeting better?

- What should we stop doing that didn't work for us or got in the way?

- What should we continue doing that worked well for us? This is an important question because it helps us identify our strengths.

Finally, review the troop meeting plan for the next meeting and make sure that everyone who will have a role is aware of the assignment and is prepared to do a good job.

While the patrol leaders' council is reviewing the meeting, the *service patrol* can put away troop gear and return the meeting room to order.

Tips for Running a Good Troop Meeting

- Prior to the meeting, review the troop meeting plan with the Scoutmaster.

- Start the meeting on time.

- Take charge of the meeting. Scouts will follow your lead.

- When you are ready to move from one part of the meeting to the next, use the Scout sign to gain the attention of all troop members.

- Stay focused on the program feature of the month.

- Keep the meeting moving. If the proceedings of one part of the meeting seem to have run out of energy, move on to the next.

- Praise patrols when they have done something well.

- When patrol members are watching, be supportive and positive in your comments to patrol leaders. If you feel the need for constructive criticism, speak with patrol leaders in private.

- Don't wear out favorite preopening or interpatrol games and activities. Try new challenges.

- Set a good example by wearing your BSA uniform to troop meetings.

- End every meeting on time.

- Review each meeting to see what can be improved in the future.

A Troop Self-Assessment

This is a self-assessment exercise designed to help highlight areas of troop success and to discover areas open to improvement.

A troop that is performing should have a high score or should have numbers that continue to improve over time.

Share the self-assessment with other youth leaders at meetings of the patrol leaders' council, and use it to explore ways to make the troop better.

Keep the self-assessment forms with the troop log so that you can compare troop performance over time.

Scoring: 3 points if the statement is always true about the troop
2 points if the statement is sometimes true about the troop
1 point if the statement is seldom true about the troop

Troop Meetings

_____ Troop meetings are planned at the monthly patrol leaders' council meeting.

_____ The patrol leaders' council uses the seven-part troop meeting plan.

_____ Troop meetings are run by the senior patrol leader.

_____ Troop meetings are fun and full of action.

_____ Skills instruction is divided into three levels of experience.

_____ Boys and adults wear appropriate uniform at all troop activities.

Patrol Method

_____ The troop has both a new-Scout patrol and a Venture patrol.

_____ Each patrol has a patrol name.

_____ Each patrol has a patrol flag.

_____ Each patrol has a patrol yell or song.

_____ Each patrol has its symbol on its equipment.

_____ Patrol members all have patrol jobs.

Camping

_____ When the troop is camping, Scouts pitch their tents in patrol campsites.

_____ Camping menus are planned and prepared by patrols.

_____ The troop camps out at least 10 days and nights each year.

_____ The troop attends a BSA-approved long-term camp.

_____ The troop offers high-adventure opportunities for its older Scouts, often in the form of a Venture patrol.

_____ All Scouts and adults are adequately trained in outdoor skills, including health and safety.

Advancement

_____ New Scouts achieve the rank of First Class during their first year in the troop.

_____ All Scouts advance at least one rank per year.

_____ Boards of review and courts of honor are held regularly.

_____ The troop helps Scouts find opportunities to earn merit badges required for advancement.

Training

_____ Newly elected youth leaders are given Introduction to Leadership training.

_____ Troop leadership training occurs at least once a year.

_____ Members of the patrol leaders' council are encouraged to participate in National Youth Leadership Training.

_____ Scoutmaster and assistant Scoutmasters are fully trained.

_____ Troop committee has completed Troop Committee Challenge or its equivalent.

Character Development

_____ Members of the troop participate in at least 10 hours of service per year.

_____ Scouts are encouraged to "do a Good Turn daily."

5
Leading the Troop Beyond the Meeting Room

Leading the Troop Beyond the Meeting Room

"Scouting," the old saying goes,

"is three-quarters *outing.*" It's in the outdoors that Scouts find the challenges and rewards of camping, hiking, and a host of other adventures. It's in the outdoors that the program of Scouting works best.

At a minimum, Scouts in the troop should be spending at least 10 days and nights outdoors each year. The weekly meetings of the troop often lay the foundations for big events in the out-of-doors. As senior patrol leader, you can bring together the possibilities of the outdoor program with the needs and interests of the Scouts in the troop.

Among the opportunities for making that happen are:

- Troop campouts
- Camporees
- Summer camps
- High-adventure treks
- Religious activities

Troop Campouts

A campout is often a program feature *big event.* Members of the patrol leaders' council planning a campout must consider what equipment and food will be needed, and how everyone will reach the campsite. Most troops will be able to provide patrols with tents, stoves, and other group gear. Patrols can be assigned the duties of developing menus, purchasing food, and getting provisions ready to pack. Food costs should be shared by all the Scouts and leaders who take part. (For more on planning and carrying out successful camping trips, see *The Boy Scout Handbook,* No. 33105, *Fieldbook,* No. 33104, and *Troop Program Features, Volumes I, II,* and *III,* Nos. 33110, 33111, and 33112.)

As with other aspects of being a senior patrol leader, you can often provide the most effective leadership by delegating responsibilities to other members of the patrol leaders' council. Provide

them with the knowledge they need, the materials they should have, and the encouragement to do their best. You will often find that they thrive on the chance to take on much of the work of preparing for and carrying out successful troop activities.

During outdoor activities, spend time with each patrol. Check with patrol leaders to ensure that the tasks on duty rosters are shared equally among all members of each patrol. Help patrol leaders see to it that everyone has a dry place to sleep and that other issues of safety and comfort are being addressed. Offer patrol leaders your full attention, and stand ready to help them if they ask for your assistance. Give patrols of younger Scouts special attention on their first outings.

Learning Together

Not every Scout who takes on the role of senior patrol leader is a crackerjack camper and outdoor expert. Perhaps yours is a newly formed troop just beginning to develop its backcountry skills, or you may have been elected to be senior patrol leader because of your abilities to organize meetings and inspire Scouts to achieve all they can.

In any case, you and the rest of the Scouts in the troop can increase your camping knowledge together while enjoying the outdoors as a group. Adult leaders of the troop, district, and council may be able to provide guidance in the best ways to live in camp and on the trail. *The Boy Scout Handbook, Fieldbook,* merit badge pamphlets, and other BSA literature can help, too.

As senior patrol leader, you can set a good example for all troop members by camping well, respecting others and the environment, and following the principles of Leave No Trace.

Camporees

Once or twice a year, most BSA districts or councils host a camporee, inviting many troops to come together for a weekend of camping fun and fellowship. Camporees are often planned around a program theme—orienteering or outdoor cooking, for example. A camporee is a chance for the patrols of the troop to show their best stuff.

The planning done by the patrol leaders' council in preparation for a camporee is similar to that required of a troop campout. Scouts can use their patrol meetings to organize their menus, make duty roster assignments, and gather their food and gear. They may also need time during troop meetings to learn and practice some of the skills they will use during camporee events and competitions.

As senior patrol leader you can support the Scouts of all the patrols with coaching and encouragement. Be available to help patrol leaders solve any problems that may arise.

Summer Camps

A local council summer camp offers troops terrific outdoor learning experiences and plenty of fun. A council camp provides the setting (open country, campsites, room to roam), basic facilities (tents, waterfront, nature center, archery and rifle ranges), equipment (boats, canoes, nature guides, recreational gear), and a trained staff (experts in aquatics, nature, woodcraft, field sports, first aid, and other Scouting skills). Scouts attending summer camp usually will be expected to bring their own clothing, sleeping bags, and personal gear.

The patrol leaders' council will develop a camp plan that allows troop members to work on advancement requirements and merit badges, to hike, to enjoy boating and swimming, and to engage in many other camp activities.

Many members of the troop will be attending summer camp for the first time. Work closely with the Scoutmaster to help these Scouts make the most of their summer camp experience. The following considerations are especially important:

- Encourage younger Scouts to take part in any first-time camper programs focusing on Tenderfoot and Second Class requirements.

- Encourage new Scouts to concentrate on mastering basic Scouting skills before working on more than one or two merit badges.

- Stay in touch with younger Scouts during summer camp. For some, this will be the first time they have been away from their families for an extended period of time. See that they have plenty to do, and help them get through symptoms of homesickness.

As at other troop functions, monitor the activities and progress of the troop's Scouts by staying in touch with each patrol leader and with the Scoutmaster. The pace of summer camp will allow you to spend plenty of time with younger Scouts and other troop members. That can lead to strengthened bonds of partnership and shared experience that can help carry the troop through the rest of the year.

Planning for Summer Camp

Getting ready for summer camp should begin at the troop's program planning meeting. The patrol leaders' council can organize program events throughout the year so that Scouts master the camping and outdoor skills they can use at summer camp.

Financing summer camp is another issue requiring long-term planning. The Scoutmaster and patrol leaders' council should work closely with the troop committee to devise the most appropriate way to fund the summer camp experience for every boy who wants to go. In some cases boys pay their own way. Other troops conduct fund-raising campaigns to gather the money to send their patrols to camp.

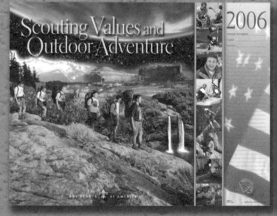

Your council may offer special precamp training sessions for senior patrol leaders, other selected youth leaders, and the troop's adult leaders. The sessions can give you a head start on making summer plans and enable you to better prepare the troop for camp.

High-Adventure Treks

High-adventure opportunities for a troop's older Scouts are limited only by the imaginations of those setting out on treks. The terrain to be explored is varied, too—whitewater rivers, mountains, deserts, lakes, forests, prairies, and oceans.

National high-adventure bases offer back-country journeys on mountain trails, along remote lakes and rivers, and across the open sea. Many local councils also offer high-adventure programs, too. The BSA publication *Passport to High Adventure,* No. 4310, lists these national and local council opportunities and is a great resource for planning any high-adventure trek.

The older Scouts in the troop may have formed a Venture patrol specializing in high-adventure activities. The patrol leaders' council and the troop's Scoutmaster must give their approval to the plans of a Venture patrol. As senior patrol leader, you may take part in Venture patrol outings, but remember that you are not in charge; a Venture patrol should always be led by the Venture patrol leader.

The way to learn good outdoor leadership is to practice leading. Get outdoors with the troop as often as you can. Begin with hikes and campouts that are manageable and within the abilities of the Scouts in the troop. As your skills and those of other Scouts increase, you can plan more challenging and rewarding adventures.

Getting Ready for the Outdoors

Any time the troop embarks on an outdoor activity, work with the patrol leaders' council to complete a trip plan. Leave a copy with someone who will notice if you do not return as expected. A trip plan will help you prepare for the event by answering the following questions:

- **Where are we going?** Decide on the destination and the intended route. Where is the starting point and ending point of the trek? In some cases it will be appropriate to include copies of a map marked with the proposed route.

- **When will we return?** If you are not back within a couple of hours of the time estimated on the trip plan, the contact people can take steps to locate you.

- **Who is going with us?** List the name of everyone who is going along.

- **Why are we going?** What is the purpose of the troop activity? The answer to this question will help you take what you need and make the most of the opportunities that present themselves.

- **What are we taking?** For most Scout outings, the outdoor essentials form the core of the items every Scout should carry. Longer trips, cold-weather journeys, and adventures involving camping out will require additional gear, clothing, and food for each Scout and for the troop. (For more on the outdoor essentials, see *The Boy Scout Handbook* and *Fieldbook*.)

- **How will we follow the principles of Leave No Trace?** Review the Leave No Trace principles and think about the ways you and the troop can stick to each one of them. Once you are in the field, keep the principles in mind and use them as reminders of the best ways to enjoy the out-of-doors.

Troop Trip Plan

Trip plan of _____

Where:
Destination _____
Route going _____
_____
Route returning_____
_____

When:
Date and time of departure _____
Date and time of return _____

Who:
Names of persons taking part _____
_____

Why:
Purpose of the trip _____
_____

What:
☑ Gear and other items to be taken:
☐ Outdoor essentials
☐ Other clothing and gear _____
_____
Permits required_____
Special equipment needs _____
Special clothing needs _____

How:
List the principles of Leave No Trace that relate to your trip. For each one, write a sentence explaining what the patrol will do to follow that principle. _____
_____
_____
_____

Leave No Trace

The Boy Scouts of America has embraced the principles of Leave No Trace as its guidelines for enjoying the outdoors in a responsible manner. The principles are designed to help outdoor users make the most of their adventures while at the same time protecting the environment and the experience of other visitors.

Principles of Leave No Trace

 Plan ahead and prepare.

 Travel and camp on durable surfaces.

 Dispose of waste properly. (Pack it in, pack it out.)

 Leave what you find.

 Minimize campfire impacts.

 Respect wildlife.

 Be considerate of other visitors.

(For more on Leave No Trace, see *The Boy Scout Handbook* and *Fieldbook*. For information on the Leave No Trace Award, see The Principles of Leave No Trace, No. 21-105.)

Evening Campfires

A highlight of many troop campouts is an evening program of stories, songs, and skits. As senior patrol leader, you will often be the logical choice to serve as master of ceremonies.

Campfire programs can offer entertainment, fellowship, and education. The setting of a campfire, the darkness that envelops it, and the fact that it is part of a larger outdoor adventure can make it an ideal time to offer messages of inspiration.

A good campfire program, like a good troop meeting, will not happen by accident. It should have elements of fun and fellowship. The program need not be an elaborate production, but a bit of planning will go a long way toward giving a campfire program purpose and direction.

The patrol leaders' council should take the lead in planning a troop's evening program and assigning its various parts to the patrols. Scouts who have attended previous camporees and summer camps may have ideas for skits, stunts, and songs. A useful guide is the BSA publication Campfire Program Planner, No. 33696.

As with all BSA events, campfire programs must be done in good taste. You and other members of the patrol leaders' council can reinforce the fact that there is no place in Scouting for poor manners; racial, ethnic, or gender slurs; or vulgarity.

The troop does not need an actual campfire to share in the enjoyment of an evening program. In fact, Scouts may find their awareness of their surroundings is enhanced by the absence of a fire.

Sitting by a river, looking out over a vista, even gathering around a candle or lantern can be every bit as effective as gazing into the embers of a campfire. If you do intend to light a blaze, follow the campfire regulations of the area where you are staying and employ all Leave No Trace principles relating to open fires.

Ready for the Rain

Of course you will have helped the troop get ready for the weather it expects to encounter on an outdoor adventure. During bad weather, you may have jumped in to assist patrols in setting up dining flies and getting their gear secured in their tents. Perhaps you have suggested to the patrol leaders that they fire up the stoves and provide hot drinks for patrol members.

Do you have some good games and other activities for troop members to pass the time when the weather turns for the worse? The BSA publications *Troop Program Features, Volumes I, II,* and *III; The Boy Scout Handbook; Fieldbook;* and other pieces of Scouting literature overflow with ideas for games, skits, skills, contests, and problem solving that can be adapted for use in tents or under a tarp. Pull together some of the best of these ahead of time for use when the rain begins to fall.

Conservation Service Projects

Scouts have always prided themselves on being good stewards of the outdoors. Today, the principles of Leave No Trace allow them to camp, hike, and take part in related outdoor activities in ways that are environmentally sound and kind to others using the same areas.

Another important lesson of Scouting is the wisdom of giving something back to the land that Scouts enjoy. A well-conceived troop conservation project benefits the environment and helps instill in Scouts the sense that they are capable of improving the world around them.

Projects vary greatly depending on the area, the skill level and enthusiasm of Scouts and their leaders, and the needs of land management personnel or private property owners. It is crucial that a project be discussed and approved well in advance by the appropriate land owner or land management agency.

A well-conceived conservation project:

- Meets a real need in protecting or restoring a natural resource.

- Has a purpose that Scouts can understand.

- Can be completed in a reasonable amount of time.

- Offers opportunities for Scouts and leaders to learn sound conservation practices.

- May be related to advancement or the requirements for a conservation award.

- Enables Scouts to come away with a sense of satisfaction in doing a Good Turn for the environment.

The BSA's *Conservation Handbook* is designed to help you and the troop undertake meaningful conservation projects. It outlines strategies for developing ongoing conservation relationships between the troop and the managers of the areas where you take part in outdoor adventures.

Religious Activities

Most troops have a troop chaplain (an adult) and a chaplain aide (youth member) who are responsible for the spiritual awareness and growth of troop members. For a troop with members of mixed beliefs, or if the beliefs of members are unknown, religious services should be interfaith in nature. However, if all members of a troop are of the same faith, it is appropriate to offer a specific worship service.

Though it is not the responsibility of a patrol leaders' council to plan and conduct worship services, it should be a part of the patrol leaders' council planning process to schedule times and places for worship to occur any time a troop outing will span a weekend.

Any time the troop is planning an outing that spans a weekend, make arrangements for the troop to have a time of worship.

How to Be a Good Senior Patrol Leader

SENIOR PATROL LEADER

How to Be a Good Senior Patrol Lead«

Think of some of the best leaders

you have known. Perhaps there is a teacher at school who seems gifted with the ability to guide people toward their goals. Maybe you are on a sports team coached by someone who inspires you to achieve the most that you can. You might have noticed the skill with which the Scoutmaster and other adult leaders move the troop along.

Now that you have become senior patrol leader, you may be asking yourself how you can be most effective in your new role. What steps can you take to lead well?

Basics of Leadership

There are almost as many methods of leadership as there are leaders. All good leaders develop their own styles, building on their successes and learning from experiences that were not so positive. Approaches to leadership that work for one person may not be at all successful for someone else. Leaders may also discover that the methods they use will change depending on the people they are leading and the challenges their groups are facing.

Even so, there are some basics of leadership that can give you a head start in developing your own approach to being a senior patrol leader. Among the most important are these:

❶ Have a good attitude.

❷ Act with maturity.

❸ Be organized.

❹ Look the part.

Have a Good Attitude

An optimistic outlook is infectious. Maintain a positive, can-do attitude, and those around you will find that they share your enthusiasm. You do not have to be noisy about it; simply be willing to do your best all the time. Instead of feeling defeated by the challenges facing the troop, set about the business of using the combined strengths of all troop members to find good solutions.

Act With Maturity

Earn the respect of those you are leading by being fair to everyone and consistent in your actions. It is important to be flexible enough to change direction when that will be best for the troop, but there is nothing more confusing than a leader who flip-flops on his decisions without clear reason. Likewise, a senior patrol leader who treats some Scouts more favorably than others will soon lose the troop's trust. Troop members will respond well to your leadership when they know what to expect from you.

Look Out for the Little Guys

As senior patrol leader, be aware of the experience of younger Scouts. Encourage them to do their best. Make it your business to help them get the most out of Scouting. Speak up any time you become aware of older Scouts picking on younger boys. The maturity you show as senior patrol leader can make it clear that yours is a troop where harassment and hazing will not be tolerated.

Be Organized

Careful preparations before meetings and troop events will pay off many times over in the success of those activities. Scouts will also receive the message that you care enough about them to put your energy into planning the best possible experiences for the entire troop.

Look the Part

Leadership comes from within, not from the shirt on your back or the patch on your shoulder. On the other hand, the Boy Scout uniform does command respect. It provides identity for troop members and can be a means of building troop spirit.

"What you do yourselves, your Scouts will do also."

Robert Baden-Powell

Set a good example for the troop by wearing the full Boy Scout uniform whenever it is appropriate:

- All Scouts proudly wear the full BSA uniform for ceremonial activities including boards of review, courts of honor, patriotic events, parades, and special occasions at troop meetings and summer camp.

- During physically active outdoor events and informal Scout meetings, troop members may wear the BSA activity uniform—troop or camp T-shirts with Scout pants or shorts.

- Scouts participating in patrol and troop conservation projects, other service work, or backcountry camping may wear work pants or jeans with their troop or camp T-shirts.

Matching Leadership Styles to Leadership Needs

Effective leaders nearly always have more than one leadership style. A key to good leadership is to match the style of leadership to the situation. For instance, a First Class Scout who has been in the troop for a year or more may require little guidance on a weekend camping trip, but a new Scout on his first campout probably will need lots of hands-on attention, encouragement, and instruction.

Among the most common styles of leadership are

- Explaining
- Demonstrating
- Guiding
- Enabling

THE EXPLAINING STYLE

Explaining is a leadership style used when patrol members are just beginning in a task or skill. They are enthusiastic but really do not have the skill or knowledge to do what needs to be done. When a patrol or an individual is at this stage, the leaders need to carefully explain what must be done, how to do it, and what the result needs to be.

THE DEMONSTRATING STYLE

When the patrol or an individual is just learning a new skill, frustration can come quickly when the skill just isn't there yet. The leader at this point needs to use the demonstrating style of leadership, showing precisely how something is to be done. He also must model the behavior expected of patrol members.

THE GUIDING STYLE

As the patrol or members get better at a task or skill, they will exhibit a growing enthusiasm and motivation. The leader's response to this should be to step back and give them plenty of room to act on their own, but be ready to coach and guide when help is needed. An example might be the patrol leader performing his responsibilities during meal preparation but remaining close by and ready to help others, if they need it. That will help guide them toward being successful.

THE ENABLING STYLE

Enabling is leadership style that can be used when skills are high to create an environment of continued success. It means the leader can delegate teaching responsibility for that task or skill to the individual or patrol. The leader recognizes that the group has reached proficiency, and he can and should express his confidence in them.

Leadership Situations

Here are five situations you may encounter as senior patrol leader, each followed by one of the many appropriate solutions. Read each situation and consider how you would handle the problem.

1. On a Weekend Campout

While visiting a patrol campsite, you notice on the patrol's duty roster that the two youngest Scouts are expected to wash dishes at every meal. What should you do?

One solution: Take the patrol leader aside and ask if the duty roster you saw is correct. If the answer is yes, find out why the same boys have been assigned dishwashing duty for the entire campout. Remind the patrol leader that a patrol is a team, and that all members of the patrol should be given equal responsibilities. Encourage him to meet with his patrol to revise the duty roster.

You may also want to check the patrol's duty roster before the next campout to be certain the patrol leader has corrected the problem.

2. At a Troop Meeting

Two patrols finish an interpatrol competition in a tie. You have only one award for first place. What do you do?

One solution: Acknowledge the tie and congratulate both patrols. Do not present the award to either patrol at this time. Make up another award and, at the next troop meeting, present an award to each patrol.

3. On a Weekend Campout

You encounter two older Scouts having an argument. You urge them to find a way to talk through their differences, but they ignore you and begin to fight. They are bigger than you are, and you cannot stop the fight alone. What should you do?

One solution: Get help from other Scouts and adult leaders. Immediately report the incident to the Scoutmaster.

4. At Troop Meetings

As a new senior patrol leader, you are disturbed that very few of the troop members wear their Scout uniforms to troop meetings. What should you do?

One solution: First, set the example by wearing the full uniform yourself. Next, discuss uniforms with the patrol leaders' council and ask the troop's other youth leaders for ways the troop can better emphasize the importance of proper uniforming.

5. A Troop Feast

The troop is planning a feast, and each patrol is responsible for a part of the meal. The patrol preparing the main course has decided to fix meat loaf. You hate meat loaf. What should you do?

One solution: As senior patrol leader, you were elected to represent the troop. You are also eager to have patrols take the initiative to decide what they want and then to follow through. Support the patrol's plans, then at the feast quietly pass on the meat loaf and enjoy a double helping of salad.

Helping the Troop Develop as a Team

Understanding how patrols in the troop develop can help you better match your leadership style to the needs of all troop members. In turn, that can encourage everyone to move toward building a troop that is able to achieve as much as it can.

Team Development

There are many theories explaining how teams like patrols and troops evolve. At the council-level National Youth Leadership Training, you will learn that teams go through a progression of stages, each requiring a different leadership approach. The Leading EDGE (Explain, Demonstrate, Guide, Enable) is the same term used to describe a process for teaching a skill, but here it describes the series of leadership behaviors you just learned.

Just as you can adjust your leadership style to match the needs of individuals, you also can address the needs of an entire team. The key is this: *Figure out what the group is missing and then provide it.*

Supporting the Troop

To discover what the troop requires from you, pay attention. Watch patrol members as they interact with one another. Listen to their comments and concerns. Notice the differences in patrols, and think about ways you can help each of them reach their full potential.

For example, members of a newly formed patrol usually are eager to be a part of the troop and will be anxious to fit in. They may be unsure about what is expected of them and will need lots of guidance. Take time to establish personal connections with each person and learn about his interests and talents. The *explaining style* and the *demonstrating style* of leadership you use with individuals can also be used with great effect when applied to newly formed groups.

A patrol that has been around for a while should have developed quite a bit of skill in resolving its difficulties and achieving many of its goals. Patrol members should be confident in their ability to perform tasks and to overcome obstacles. They have a sense of pride in belonging to a successful patrol, and they enjoy working together for the good of the troop. The trust and respect they have for one another is also high.

You can support experienced patrols by seeing to it that they have everything they require to continue succeeding. Those resources may be in the form of materials, camping gear, or knowledge, especially information you can share from meetings of the patrol leaders' council. Recognize individuals for their accomplishments, and encourage open communication. You may find that the *guiding style* and *enabling style* of leadership are just right for bringing out the best in veteran patrols.

Providing Leadership to the Troop

- Rely on the Scout Oath and Law as you make ethical choices in troop leadership. Shared values are a foundation of any team. The Scout Law and Oath are expressions of the BSA's values.

- Offer a vision of success. The troop's annual program plan is a blueprint for exciting activities and outdoor adventures. Use it to focus Scouts' energies and enthusiasm.

- Recognize that some Scouts are moving faster than others. Give additional assistance to Scouts who are taking more time to learn skills and to gain Scouting experience. Offer advanced Scouts added responsibilities and leadership positions.

- Model the kind of behavior and achievement you expect from everyone in your troop. Be what you want them to be. Have high expectations for yourself and expect the best in others.

- Acknowledge differences. Look for ways to draw on individual strengths of Scouts to the advantage of the entire troop. Develop trust by keeping the interests of troop members in mind.

- Make meetings count. Get outdoors and have adventures. Working through the patrol leaders' council, develop an exciting program plan, then carry it out.

- Respect and value others. Help each Scout feel that he has something important to contribute to the success of his patrol and troop.

Overcoming Troop Disappointments

Now and then a troop may become discouraged. Perhaps Scouts are discovering the reality of the challenges facing them. A camp-out or other planned activity that didn't go very well may cause some Scouts to become frustrated.

You will be tested as senior patrol leader when the spirits of troop members are down. When that happens, draw upon your abilities to communicate clearly, listen actively, and encourage open discussions. Recognize patrol accomplishments and offer encouragement and reassurance to those Scouts who are making efforts to achieve. Reflection can be an effective tool for you to discover what is at the root of troop members' discontent and for helping Scouts find their own solutions to the situation.

Celebrating Success

Patrols in the troop will achieve significant milestones, or even complete their time together as a tight-knit group. Members of some patrols may be moving on to form a Venture crew, for example, or members of a new-Scout patrol may have reached a level of experience and advancement to be ready to join the regular patrols of the troop.

Whatever the case, celebrate the many accomplishments that troop members have enjoyed during their time together. Documenting patrol and troop histories with a scrapbook or photo album can be an enjoyable way to create an overview of all that the Scouts have accomplished.

Conflict Resolution

Conflicts can occur when people disagreeing with each other seem unable to find a reasonable compromise. The roots of these disagreements can arise from many sources, including differences in personality, values, and perceptions.

As senior patrol leader, you must handle the differences that arise among members of the troop. Conflicts may be minor, or they may fester into something that can damage troop spirit and the ability of the Scouts to work together effectively.

Avoiding

Avoiding a problem will seldom make it go away, but there are times when it is best to let others work out their differences on their own. By using the skills of effective listening, you should have a good feel for the quality of the relationships among troop members and can decide when it will be of value for you to do something to help resolve a disagreement.

An important time for you to step in is when troop members themselves are side-stepping a problem by shying away from the steps that would lead to a resolution of a disagreement. They may have decided simply not to talk about it, but without communication there can be no progress.

Conflict Resolution

Your response

to a perceived

conflict will

probably take

one of three forms:

❶ Avoiding

❷ Compromising

❸ Problem solving

Compromising

In solving a conflict by compromise, both parties must be willing to give up something to gain something more. Reaching that point may require the assistance of a negotiator—often you, the senior patrol leader.

Problem Solving

The most effective way to resolve conflicts is for all parties to explain their points of view and to become convinced that they should make a real effort to solve the problem. As in compromising, a negotiator may serve as a guide to help them resolve their differences.

The Senior Patrol Leader as Conflict Negotiator

When two members of the troop are in disagreement with one another, you can often find a workable solution by using many of the same skills that are effective when the actions of a single person are unacceptable. Stay calm. Use open-ended questions to get everyone to explain his understanding of the problem. Encourage each person to see the situation from other points of view, then enlist the aid of all parties working together to find a solution that is acceptable to everyone.

Start, Stop, Continue Assessment Tool

Start, Stop, Continue is a series of questions designed to help troop members assess an event or activity that has just occurred and explore some of the values that activity offers. The troop can then take the outcome and focus on reapplication and future events. Troops that use SSC are less likely to end up with an emphasis on what went wrong than when using other assessment tools. In its simplest form, SSC is three questions:

1. What should we start doing that would make us more successful?

2. What should we stop doing that is not working or is a barrier to our success?

3. What should we continue to do because it was a significant reason for our success?

For major events and when you are a more experienced leader, the group can explore the why of each question. The answers often will help to reinforce the values of the Scout Oath and Law in the experience.

Some key points for using the SSC assessment tool:

- Everyone has the right to express his thoughts.

- Each person has the choice of talking or remaining silent.

- No one may interrupt the person speaking, and there is no room for put-downs or making fun of someone.

- Gathering input here is key, but it is not always necessary to evaluate and reach consensus. The patrol leaders' council may be the right place to review the input and apply a solution.

- Do not allow the discussion to become negative or focus on individuals.

To end the discussion, summarize the most important points that were mentioned. When appropriate, the troop scribe should keep a record to be shared at the next patrol leaders' council meeting. Be positive throughout the session and as you bring it to a close.

Communication Skills

Communicating effectively is more than just visiting with someone, especially when you are giving and receiving important information. At a troop meeting or during a troop activity, you will sometimes have the challenge of giving detailed information to Scouts in such a way that all of them clearly understand the message.

Giving Information

Assume you have just met with the Scoutmaster to outline the agenda for the troop's planning conference. Now you need to share that information with members of the patrol leaders' council.

- Before you begin, take a moment to organize your thoughts. You may want to write a few notes to remind yourself of the points you want to cover.

- Have the council members gather in a place free of distractions. If you are outdoors on a bright day, turn so that you, rather than the listeners, are facing the sun. Do not begin until you have everyone's attention. You can use the Scout sign as a signal that it is time for everyone to stop other discussions and focus on the business at hand.

- Speak clearly. Make eye contact with your listeners. As you finish explaining each item, ask if there are any questions.

- If possible, write the most important points on a flip chart or chalkboard.

- Repeat facts such as dates, times, and places.

- Ask the troop scribe to make notes of the discussion.

- Ask them to report to you the important information.

Receiving Information

Communication is a two-way street. When you are in a position to receive information, give it your full attention. Create an atmosphere for communication to happen by doing the following:

- Give the speaker your full attention.

- Write down points of information—dates, times, locations, etc.

- If you are unclear about anything, ask questions.

Effective Listening

As you can see from the discussion of giving and receiving information, effective listening is essential to good communication. Effective listening is also a skill that each of us can learn and can constantly improve.

❶ **Effective listening is vital for forming relationships, finding solutions, and developing troop spirit.**

❷ **Effective listening can be a tool for turning a negative situation into a positive one.**

Most of us love to hear the sounds of our own voices. In conversations, we may think more about what we are going to say next than about what is being said by others. When you are in conversations with members of the troop, though, practice good listening by paying close attention to what others are saying and also to what they are leaving unsaid. Notice their tone of voice and watch their body language. Try to listen without passing judgment.

Be aware, too, of how you are feeling while you listen. Are you chilly, hungry, sleepy, too hot, too cold, or late for another meeting? Is the speaker's message something you do not want to hear? Any of these factors can have an impact on your attention span. If you are upset, angry, or worried, that can affect your ability to listen well.

Noticing how you feel can help you better grasp what others are saying. The adjustment you make might simply be a matter of focusing more on a speaker's message. Often, though, it may require calling a time-out so that you can put on a sweater, have a bite to eat, take care of distracting matters, or let your emotions cool down. When you get back together with the speaker, the conditions may be much more inviting to good listening.

Of course, you cannot tailor every listening situation to be ideal. Now and then you will find yourself in discussions with others when communication is difficult. Continually practice effective listening, though, and you will find that it can be a powerful tool for solving problems, settling disputes, building troop spirit, and making you a more effective leader.

Follow-up

Communicating well is a constant goal of a senior patrol leader. Sometimes, though, a patrol leader is absent from a patrol leaders' council meeting. Sometimes plans you have discussed with the council must be changed at the last minute. The follow-up steps you take in these situations can ensure that effective communication continues:

- Make a list of the phone numbers and e-mail addresses of the members of the patrol leaders' council. Use it to contact everyone if you need to provide them with information outside of a scheduled meeting.

- Give troop members as much advance notice as possible concerning upcoming activities. If you wait until the last minute, some Scouts may have scheduling conflicts.

- Keep the troop calendar updated with accurate information on troop events and activities.

- Discuss the troop's activities with your parents or guardian. They need to know your schedule, and they may be an important resource for ideas and support.

- Plan, plan, plan. Fill out a planning work sheet on every activity.

Dealing With Inappropriate Behavior

The Scouting program offers young people opportunities to learn and grow in a setting where they can feel that they enjoy the acceptance and support of others. Hazing, harassment, name-calling, and bullying have no place in Scouting and will not be tolerated. Likewise, cheating, stealing, lying, cursing, vandalism, fighting, and other forms of inappropriate behavior must be firmly addressed by a Scout troop.

Scouting is built upon the boy-led troop and boy-led patrol. As senior patrol leader, you set an example for the behavior of everyone in the troop. When you see that a member of the troop is overstepping the boundaries of the code of conduct spelled out in the Scout Oath and Law, it is your responsibility to step aside with that Scout and discuss with him why his behavior is not acceptable.

Serious or recurring inappropriate behavior should be reported to the Scoutmaster. The patrol leaders' council may become involved in discussing certain behavioral problems. Disruptive behavior on the part of an individual Scout may be referred to the Scoutmaster and troop committee who will, in turn, involve the Scout's parents or guardians in a cooperative effort to resolve the issue.

"The thing is to cooperato happily in the process which develops discipline and obedience in the doing of small things while we are young. Then, when our turn comes to do big things, discipline will help to ensure accomplishment."

—*James E. West, BSA's Chief Scout Executive, 1910–1943*

The Troop Leadership Team

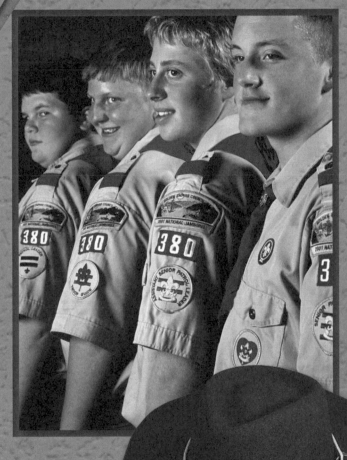

The Troop Leadership Team

A Boy Scout troop is a small democracy. With the Scoutmaster's guidance, Scouts form themselves into patrols, plan the troop's program, and bring it to life. For that to happen, a troop relies upon Scouts serving in positions of responsibility. The key youth leaders of the troop make up a patrol leaders' council.

Patrol Leaders' Council

The patrol leaders' council plans and runs the troop's program and activities and gives long-range direction with an annual planning meeting that lays out the troop's calendar for the year. The patrol leaders' council also meets each month to fine-tune upcoming troop meetings and activities. They get together for a few moments after each troop meeting to review the plans for the next troop meeting and make any adjustments to ensure its success.

The senior patrol leader conducts meetings of the patrol leaders' council. Patrol leaders present the ideas and concerns of their patrols, help develop the troop's overall program, then take the council's decisions to the rest of the troop members.

The Scoutmaster attends patrol leaders' council meetings as a coach and an informational resource. As much as possible, he allows the Scouts to run the meetings and make the decisions, stepping in with suggestions and guidance when that will enhance the program for the troop, the patrols, and individuals. The Scoutmaster retains veto power over decisions of the council but should need to exercise it only on rare occasions when the plans of the patrol leaders' council would violate BSA policy or could lead to a situation that might jeopardize the safety and well-being of troop members.

Other Troop Positions

Depending on the size and needs of a troop, a number of other leadership positions may be filled. Except for assistant senior patrol leaders and troop guides, Scouts serving in troop positions will continue to be active members of their patrols. With the assistance of the Scoutmaster, you as senior patrol leader will select the Scout who will hold each position.

- Assistant senior patrol leader (large troops may have several)

- Troop guide (one for each new-Scout patrol)

- Troop quartermaster
- Troop historian
- Troop chaplain aide
- Troop librarian
- Troop scribe
- Instructors
- Den chiefs
- Webelos den chief
- Junior assistant Scoutmaster
- Order of the Arrow troop representative

Filling Positions of Leadership

An essential step in creating any successful team is selecting the right people to serve in positions of leadership. The patrol leaders' council of the troop will be made up in large part by patrol leaders elected by members of their patrols. It is up to you to fill the other positions of troop leadership. Careful selections can give the troop solid guidance and enthusiastic leadership for months to come.

As you begin thinking about the people you will appoint to play leadership roles in the troop, keep these pointers in mind:

- Take all the time you need to consider the responsibilities of each position and the qualifications of each Scout, then make the right match. These positions do not need to be filled immediately.

- Be fair to everyone. Consider each Scout's advancement record, Scout spirit, and commitment to his patrol and troop. Take into account strengths, weaknesses, experience, and service to Scouting.

- Do not allow friendships with some troop members to interfere with your efforts to select the best person for each position.

- Discuss your ideas with the Scoutmaster.

Assistant Senior Patrol Leader

The assistant senior patrol leader should be a strong ally for you, someone who can be relied upon to help the troop move forward. You will keep him fully informed about what is going on with the troop and can use him as a sounding board when you must make tough decisions.

Among his specific duties, the assistant senior patrol leader trains and provides direction to the troop quartermaster, scribe, historian, librarian, instructors, and Order of the Arrow representative. He will also take charge of the troop whenever you are not available. During his tenure as assistant senior patrol leader he is not a member of a patrol, but he may participate in the high-adventure activities of a Venture patrol. Large troops may have more than one assistant senior patrol leader, each appointed by the senior patrol leader.

Troop Guide

The troop guide is both a leader and a mentor to the members of the new-Scout patrol. He should be an older Scout who holds at least the First Class rank and can work well with younger Scouts. He helps the patrol leader of the new-Scout patrol in much the same way that a Scoutmaster works with a senior patrol leader to provide direction, coaching, and support.

The troop guide is not a member of another patrol but may participate in the high-adventure activities of a Venture patrol.

Quartermaster

The quartermaster is the troop's supply boss. He keeps an inventory of troop equipment and sees that the gear is in good condition. He works with patrol quartermasters as they check out equipment and return it, and at meetings of the patrol leaders' council reports on the status of equipment in need of replacement or repair. In carrying out his responsibilities, he may have the guidance of a member of the troop committee.

Scribe

The scribe is the troop's secretary. Though not a voting member, he attends meetings of the patrol leaders' council and keeps a record of the discussions. He cooperates with the patrol scribes to record attendance and dues payments at troop meetings and to maintain troop advancement records. If the troop has an Internet Web site, the scribe can help keep it up-to-date. A member of the troop committee may assist him with his work.

Historian

The historian collects and preserves troop photographs, news stories, trophies, flags, scrapbooks, awards, and other memorabilia and makes materials available for Scouting activities, the media, and troop history projects.

Librarian

The troop librarian oversees the care and use of troop books, pamphlets, magazines, audiovisuals, and merit badge counselor lists. He checks out these materials to Scouts and leaders and maintains records to ensure that everything is returned. He may also suggest the acquisition of new literature and report the need to repair or replace any current holdings.

Instructor

Each instructor is an older troop member proficient in a Scouting skill. He must also have the ability to teach that skill to others. An instructor typically teaches subjects that Scouts are eager to learn—especially those such as first aid, camping, and backpacking—that are required for outdoor activities and rank advancement. A troop can have more than one instructor.

Chaplain Aide

The chaplain aide assists the troop chaplain (usually an adult from the troop committee or the chartered organization) in serving the religious needs of the troop. He ensures that religious holidays are considered during the troop's program planning process and promotes the BSA's religious emblems program.

Den Chief

The den chief works with a den of Cub Scouts and with their adult leaders. He takes part in den meetings, encourages Cub Scout advancement, and is a role model for younger boys. Serving as den chief can be a great first leadership experience for a Scout.

Webelos Den Chief

A Webelos den chief can help plan and assist with the leadership of Webelos den meetings and field activities. He can lead songs and stunts, and encourage Webelos Scouts to progress into the Boy Scout troop.

Junior Assistant Scoutmaster

A Scout at least 16 years of age who has shown outstanding leadership skills may be appointed by the senior patrol leader, with the advice and consent of the Scoutmaster, to serve as a junior assistant Scoutmaster. These young men (a troop may have more than one junior assistant Scoutmaster) follow the guidance of the Scoutmaster in providing support and supervision to other boy leaders in the troop. Upon his 18th birthday, a junior assistant Scoutmaster will be eligible to become an assistant Scoutmaster.

Order of the Arrow Troop Representative

The Order of the Arrow representative serves as a communication link between the troop and the local Order of the Arrow lodge. By enhancing the image of the Order as a service arm to the troop, he promotes the Order, encourages Scouts to take part in all sorts of camping opportunities, and helps pave the way for older Scouts to become involved in high-adventure programs. The OA troop representative assists with leadership skills training. He reports to the assistant senior patrol leader.

One of the most satisfying aspects of leading a troop is sharing that leadership. Give troop leaders specific responsibilities, make sure they understand what is expected of them, and provide them with the guidance and resources they need. You will soon discover that the troop is exciting, active, and lively, and that you did not have to do it all yourself.

Additional Training Resources

Scouting takes pride in giving its youth leaders unique leadership training. As senior patrol leader, you may have the opportunity to participate in some or all of the following training sessions.

Introduction to Leadership

This is the first step of leadership training. The Scoutmaster will conduct it within a few days after you are elected to be senior patrol leader. Lasting not more than an hour, it will cover your responsibilities as senior patrol leader and upcoming events in the troop.

Troop Leadership Training

A three-module, three-hour training conference conducted by you and the Scoutmaster, Troop Leadership Training will reinforce the patrol method and encourage members of the patrol leader's council to set goals for their patrols and the troop.

National Youth Leadership Training

Many local councils throughout the country offer a weeklong youth leadership training. Conducted in the outdoor settings of council camps, these courses supplement training done within a troop and introduce senior patrol leaders and patrol leaders to more advanced leadership skills.

National Advanced Youth Leadership Experience

The BSA's National Council hosts National Advanced Youth Leadership Experience during the summer at Philmont Training Center. NAYLE is a scenario course that allows participants to apply NYLT leadership skills in a wilderness environment. Participants must have completed the council National Youth Leadership Training and be nominated by the Scout executives of their local councils.

National Leadership Seminars

National Leadership Seminars focusing on the skills and attributes of leadership are hosted by the Order of the Arrow. Youth leaders invited to attend these weekend events must be at least 15 years of age or be serving as officers in their council's Order of the Arrow lodge.

Other Resources for Senior Patrol Leaders

Scouting will provide many resources you can use as you fulfill your senior patrol leader responsibilities. For guidance and support, you can count on the Scoutmaster, assistant Scoutmasters, and members of the troop committee. A wealth of BSA literature is available to help you become an effective leader and to make the most of your Scouting experience. The following publications are of special interest to senior patrol leaders:

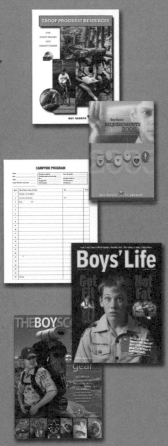

- *The Boy Scout Handbook,* No. 33105

- *Patrol Leader Handbook,* No. 32502A

- *Boy Scout Requirements* (current year), No. 33215

- *Troop Program Resources,* No. 33588

- *Troop Program Features, Volumes I, II,* and *III,* Nos. 33110, 33111, 33112

- Troop Planning Work Sheet (from *Troop Program Features*)

- *Troop Leadership Training,* No. 34306A

- *Fieldbook,* No. 33104

- *Boys' Life* magazines

- *Boy Scout Songbook*, No. 33224A

- Troop and patrol rosters

- Copies of troop rules and policies

- Activity calendar (troop, district, council, chartered organization)

- First Class First Year Tracking Sheet, No. 34118A

- Campfire Program Planner Sheet, No. 33696

- BSA Supply catalog

- Participant notebooks for youth leader training courses

In Conclusion

This book began by congratulating you on having accepted one of the best jobs in Scouting—that of being a senior patrol leader. Eventually the time will come when you will have completed your term of office and will pass leadership of the troop to someone else. When that happens, you should be able to look back with pride at all that you and the troop have accomplished while you were wearing the senior patrol leader's patch.

No doubt the troop will have become stronger because you were there. Certainly you and the other troop members will have memories of lots of fine adventures and other Scouting activities. Together, you will have met many challenges along the way and will have worked as a team to find solutions to all sorts of situations.

Scouting will present you with other leadership opportunities, both as a youth and as a young adult. The troop will continue to grow and thrive, building on the strong foundation you will have left and bringing in the fresh ideas and energy of new senior patrol leaders and new members.

You will also find that the leadership skills you have learned as a senior patrol leader are going to serve you well in school, in the community, and in other settings beyond the BSA. By asking you to accept the responsibility for guiding a troop, Scouting gives you hands-on opportunities to learn and practice essential methods of leading people. Wherever you go in life and whatever you do, those skills will go with you. Time and again they are going to help you make a real difference, both in your life and in the lives of others.

Acknowledgments

The Boy Scouts of America gratefully acknowledges the contributions of the following people for their help in the preparing of *The Senior Patrol Leader Handbook*.

- Scouts and Scouters throughout the country who participated in focus groups, photography efforts, and manuscript reviews
- Members of the National Council's Literature Review Committee: Bob Longoria, chairman; Jim Grossman; Mike O'Quinn; Larry Warlick

National Office Publishing Team

Project director
Joe C. Glasscock, Boy Scout Division, BSA

Account executive
Maria C. Dahl, Custom Communication Division, BSA

Author
Robert Birkby, Eagle Scout and mountaineer

Editor/copy editor
Beth McPherson, Custom Communication Division, BSA

Proofreader
Karen M. Kraft, Custom Communication Division, BSA

Design/art direction
Julie Moore, managing designer/art director;
   Custom Communication Division, BSA

Glenn Howard, assistant art director

Imaging artist
Melinda VanLone, Custom Communication Division, BSA

Prepress specialist
Joanne McGuire, Custom Communication Division, BSA

Print coordinator
Kimberly Kailey, Custom Communication Division, BSA

Photography
Michael Roytek, photography manager;
   Custom Communication Division, BSA

Randy Piland, freelance photographer

Kellie Pence, photography assistant;
   Custom Communication Division, BSA

Notes

Notes

Notes

Notes

Notes

Notes

Notes

Notes

Notes

Notes

Notes

Notes

Notes